WORTH
CONTEMPLATING

T0128789

WORTH
CONTEMPLATING

A Treasury Of Poems
Reflections And Views

Worrel A. Edwards

authorHOUSE®

AuthorHouse™
1663 Liberty Drive
Bloomington, IN 47403
www.authorhouse.com
Phone: 1-800-839-8640

Published by AuthorHouse   07/13/2012

ISBN: 978-1-4772-4133-2 (sc)
ISBN: 978-1-4772-4132-5 (e)

Library of Congress Control Number: 2012912418

Contents

Chapter 1: Contemplating

Chapter 2: Reflections

Chapter 3: Views

Acknowledgements

First I must give thanks to God, the father of my lord and saviour Jesus Christ, who inspired me to write my first book. I am grateful to everyone who contributed and supported me. I thank my wife Donna, my daughter Priscilla, My best friend and biggest supporter, Denise Francis; My cousin William Ashley, thank you for your words of encouragement and for your amazing job designing the cover. Thanks to Beverley McKenzie for your dedication, hard work, patience, guidance and expertise which helped me to achieve this goal. Finally, thanks to Author house.

Foreword

This book of inspirational verses is authored by Worrel Edwards, a very spiritual, enduring and motivated person, a man of profound faith in God and humanity. I met Worrel, and his wife, Donna, some time ago, and we discovered that we had a lot in common—reading, music, family, travel, and meeting people. Worrel spoke about his passion for writing, and also about his idea for publishing spiritual poems and verses. He offered to let me read a few of the verses, and I found myself deeply moved by his words.

This book deals with friendship, religion, work, as well as other day-to-day issues. You will feel uplifted and rested when you read the words before you. Once you have read this book, I am sure you will recommend it to members of your family, friends, and even your church family.

I would like to congratulate Worrel for having come to the end of his long journey in making this book a great success.

Arlene P. August
Toronto, Ontario
May 2012

Contemplating

GOD is LOVE

Chapter 1

Changes

I have a decision to make
That will change people's lives,
There is no one but myself,
That can make these changes,
It may hurt the people I love.

I cannot change the world,
That, I've been told;
I cannot please the world,
That, I have learned;
But I can change my life.

Some will understand,
Some will never understand;
There is a time when you have to make changes,
Brothers and sisters will curse you,
Friends will blame you,
It's the price you have to pay.

I know the day will come,
When I have to choose,
Between man and God,
I see the light of righteousness surround me,
It's the only love that I can see.

Life is a maze

I see life as one big maze
With lots of turns,
Some make it through,
For they seek righteousness
Along the way,
With God being their guide;

Wide is the gateway to destruction,
Narrow is the gateway to life,
Many fail, for the light they seek,
Is the light of silver and gold
They get lost in the maze of life.

I live and I see the struggle
That the people face day by day,
I didn't know,
It was the same everywhere,
In the maze of life.

Too blind

There is a war going on,
Many people are too blind
To see this war,
The Devil takes control of their sight,
So everything seems alright.

Every religious leader says,
Their religion is the right one,
There goes the religious war,
People are confused,
For the Devil's light is shining bright.

There is no other love,
Just one universal love.
We are one in truth,
All separation is misconception,
It's temporary blindness.

Walk in darkness no more,
For there is only one God,
Don't believe everything they say.
See the light for yourself,
For the truth is within you.

Be on guard

I see confusion and frustration
All around us;
Life has no value
It is only money that counts,
In a system that is built on hate,
Where love is evacuated.

Bitterness in our heart
Is tearing us apart,
So be smart,
Try and see the world,
Through the eyes of a child
And you will see what true love is all about.

Don't be blind
To the wickedness of this world,
Satan is in full control of this wickedness,
Don't let him get a hold on you,
Be on your guard,
Never let it down.

Living in a society

Living in a society,
Where money becomes
Our first priority,
It's like a worldwide establishment.
In every city,
And every village,
Money is the talk.

What about God?
You should seek him first
And everything will be alright.
Love the Lord your God,
With all your heart and your soul,
And all your strength;

He is the answer
To all problems,
It can't be too small,
It cannot be too large,
Make him your first priority;
Humble yourself under God's mighty hand,
That he may lift you up.

Colour of love

God is black
God is white
Why do we worry about
The colour of His skin?
Racism will lead you to reject salvation.

Love accepts all colours
For the world is colour
Love accepts the world
The colour of love,
Is the colour of the world

God is a God of every colour
Class and race,
God is a rainbow God,
It doesn't matter,
Where you're from, rich or poor.

Too much fighting,
Over the colour of His skin,
Remember it's only
One God and one human race
So let us all embrace.

All things are temporary

All things are temporary,
Nothing is forever, because it is nothing;
It is not for you to hold on to,
Nothing, is what's given to mankind,
Everything that we see is just for a while,
We must learn to enjoy everything
That is here for us each day.

It is nothing, it's everywhere,
You cannot take it with you;
It's like the air we breathe,
You can feel it,
You can enjoy it,
But can never hold onto it,
So are all things.

This is the reason why
The things you would die for,
Means nothing to God,
He sees all things as nothing,
For all things before him is meaningless,
Except your soul.

The poor man story

The poor man's story has been told,
With the gun again;
Poverty breeds crime and suffering,
This is not the answer;
God help us all.
You can choose love over hate,
You can choose peace over war,
You have to make a choice.

There has to be a solution;
The grave is never satisfied,
The gun could never be the answer
My brothers and sisters,
We've been brainwashed far too long,
Let's sit and talk to each other.

We have to educate ourselves,
About the system that make us haters,
We have to overcome their deception,
Give back the gun to the gun makers
Let them keep their destruction.

We must start caring for each other,
Light skin, dark skin,
We are one people,
The texture of your hair,
The shape of your nose
Makes no difference,
We are one, just give love a try.
Unity is strength.

Let love be our guide

We were taught:
'To be a better human being,
You must be rich.'
That's the philosophy of mankind,
Not the philosophy of God.

Money and power,
Could never make you a better person,
It is love for your fellow man,
That makes you a better human being.

Love one another,
Treat each other with respect,
Remember the poor man and the rich man
Are equal in pain and suffering, we are one.

Let love be our guide,
Let's put away our selfish pride,
And ride the tide of love.

Confused

In a world where money
Becomes the sole survivor
Many are confused.
And many are lost.
I am troubled to see how blind we are.

Living in this world of competition
We forget what love means.
Everyone is reaching out to touch
The great material things in life

I look around to find a brother
That is not troubled
But everyone has a story to tell;
It's all about money.
What a spell, straight to hell.

Confused world,
Confused mind,
Confused world,
Confused mind;

Stand firm

Keep safe what has been
Entrusted to your care,
Avoid the profane talk and foolish arguments,
Which some people wrongly call knowledge.

STAND FIRM! Do what is right,
STAND FIRM! Live in the light,
STAND FIRM! Never let your guard down.

Some have claimed to possess gifts from God,
And as a result, they have lost the way of faith,
Be careful children,
The Master is watching you.

Put not your trust in silver and gold,
But in God, who gives generously,
Be ready to share with others,
And have a future of happiness.

Surrender not your soul

The Devil is very generous,
He will give you anything
For your soul,
So be careful what you do
When a gun is next to you.

There is no justice with a gun,
Why shoot your brother down;
There is no justice with a gun,
Why shoot your sister down.

When you hold a gun in your hand,
There is a power that comes over you,
That makes you feel that you can do
Anything you want to do;

The Devil has power in his hands,
He is very tricky
And will do anything
To have you under his spell,
To send you to hell!

Lost mind

Why does the poor
Do evil against the poor?
They can't find food to eat
And no resting place to lay their heads,
Yet they find time to hate and kill
Every single day;

Even though they give you a smile
Evil consumes their mind,
They will talk and laugh with you
Then plot against you,
To destroy everything that you have
Without any guilt or pity;

These workers of iniquity
Filled with jealousy,
Trapped in their own filthy minds,
That are poisoned by greed
And blinded by darkness,
The light of love has never existed before them,
Blinded by their wickedness.

If god is love

If God is love,
If God is good,
If God created all man,
If God's law is the law of truth,
If God loves peace,
If God's love is everlasting,
If God sent his son,
To teach and preach love,
That all man should live in unity:

Why do we hate?
Why do we kill?
Why do we believe one
Is better than the other?
Why do we embrace war?
Why do we say, 'I kill in the name of God'?
Why do we break the law of love?
Why do we break the law of life?
The law of life is love.

If freedom is equality
All man should be treated equal.
Equality is that every man is a man,
And have the freedom to do as
Every other man can do, without prejudice,
When this world is colour blind,
Then true love will exist in the world
And that is true freedom,
Freedom is a child that plays with their friends;
Never seeing the colour of their skins, only seeing a friend;
For his eyes are the eyes of God.

They try

They try to keep me down,
But I refuse to give up the fight,
Even thou the odds are against me.

I will never lay down my arms,
I will never surrender
To the hands of the wicked.
You can chain my hands and feet,
But you will never chain this mind.

Stronger I will be
All the days of my life,
For my strength is in the Lord,
Love is my defence against hate,
In this, constant battle that I fight.

Sometimes it seems impossible,
But with God by my side,
Nothing is impossible.
Good will prevail over evil
And I will come out victorious in the end.

Troubled time

Waking up each morning
With pain in my heart,
Knowing I'll be facing another day
Without food on my table,
Children are crying,
My heart is aching
And there's nothing I can do.

Everywhere I go,
It's the same answer,
'No help wanted.'
This feeling makes me haunted,
So many bad things go through my mind;
It's the good Lord, who carries me through
Each and every day;

Sometimes I feel like
It's a hopeless situation,
When I think about what is going on
Throughout the world,
Is this the end of time?
For things seem to be the same everywhere I go.

Give me your blessing

Changes in life are so hard to do,
I want to stop doing the things
That I know is not right,
And those are the things that I find myself
Doing over and over again;

Have you ever taken some time
Just you alone?
Thinking about all the things
That you have been through?
If you haven't, you should try it.

All those mistakes we had made,
We have learned from them;
Yet we make the same mistakes all over again,
For some people it's once bitten twice shy;
We are not perfect,
The journey of life is like the four seasons.

There is hope

There is hope in every man
That seeks God's love.
Street of hate,
Street of love.

There is a thin line between love and hate,
You've got to make a choice
Between good and evil.
There is a hell and a heaven
It's up to you to believe.

God's love stands for all,
Whether you're rich or poor,
Black or white,
God's love stands for all,
He is just, to every one
Walk in his way and you will be alright.

You can choose
To walk on the street of hate,
Or you can choose
To walk on the street of love
Where God's love shines,
Every man that walks on that street finds happiness.

The World

The world is turning upside down,
The world is running out of love,
There is a global war going on,
It's all about might; it's not about truths and rights,
People want to be free,
Instead of living in a world of confusion;

There will be no peace
Until we know the meaning of love
Equal rights and justice, for one and all;
It's a global problem.
Leaders must talk.

Freedom means equality
To every race and creed.
Where there is no equality to the races,
There will be racial discrimination,
For the hearts of men are filled with hate.

Lies can divide any nation
But the truth can set them free,
When we can see each other as equals
As God Almighty sees us in His sight,
Everything will be alright.

War fails

The human race
Has turned away from God.
As the heaven
Is high above the earth,
So great is His mercy
Toward the human race.
Who is like God, for there is no other?

It's only God,
Who can save the human race,
For there is no problem
Too big or too small
That God can't solve.
Put your trust in God,
He will deliver you from the pit of corruption.

Too much innocent blood;
No war can save the human race.
Using war to save the human race,
Is the work of the Devil,
For it's only God who can save the human race.

The unknown

How does my mind work?
Where do my thoughts come from?
Why do I worry, why do I cry?
How do I know good from bad?
What is love, what is hate?
It is the unknown.

Who is the unknown?
The one who woke you up this morning,
Gave you a sound mind
Let you move and exist,
He is the spirit that lives within,
We are is temple;
He fills us, never dictates to us.

He gave us free will,
That we can do the things
We want to do,
All we have to do is honour Him,
Live by His will, by doing good to each other,
Love one another and serve Him.

What a love

Can you imagine the pain that Mary felt
Watching Jesus hanging from the cross?
Not even tears could ease her pain,
But she could hear him say,
"Father forgive them,
For they know not what they have done."
It was love, true love to the end,
How can you forget that love?
It's the greatest bond between a mother and child,
Don't you try to take away a mother's child.

Religion

Religion, religion, religion;
Religion divides the world.
Like a wolf in sheep clothing,
They hide behind their religion;
If there is one God, and God is love,
How can you divide God?
How can you divide love?

God's love is sincere,
God's love is constant,
Cannot be changed.
Too many people
Fall in love with religion, instead of God,
Seek the truth about God Almighty,
And you will see that religion is a lie.

Out of religion comes hate and inferior,
Out of love comes equality and freedom,
God made all men equal and free,
Out of politics comes greed and poverty.
Religion and politics together equal destruction.
Mankind gets confused and lost,
All that matters is God Almighty, nothing else.

Try and see love

Can you tell me
The colour of a man skin?
Is it black?
Is it brown?
Is it white?
I want to know.
Can you tell me
The colour of a man skin?

From a distance,
The ocean looks blue,
Can you tell me
The colour of the sky?
Is it gray?
Is it blue?
Is it white?
I want to know,
Can you tell me the colour?

Can you tell me?
The colour of love,
Is it red?
Is it yellow?
Is it green?
I want to know,
Can you tell me?
The colour of love,
Not everything you think you see,
Is really what you see.

It takes a minute

It takes a minute, to change one's life,
I am not giving up;
It takes a minute, to rearrange one's life,
I am not giving up.
It is the greatest mystery on this journey,
The unknown second,
Today you are up tomorrow you are down,
No matter what you are going through,
There is always a break through.

Even when the odds are against you,
Don't lose hope,
Have faith in God.
He is always watching over you,
The hardest fall in life
Will bring out the best in you.

How poor can the poor man get?
Giving up,
That's how poor he will get,
But if he never gives up,
He will never be defeated,
God will never give a man more than he can bear.

Question

Question, question,
Where are all the answers?
God knows the answers to all the questions,
That have never been answered.

You can kill today,
And get away tomorrow from the laws of men,
But you can't get away from the law of God;
He sees all things,
He is the judge of all.

He is the God of today,
He is the God of tomorrow,
He is the beginning and the end,
You better be careful what you do;
God is watching over you.

Whenever you do wrong,
Remember that you can't
Get away from your conscience;
For what you sow,
You will surely reap.

Love of god

What makes me happy?
Pleasure leaves me unhappy.
Happiness I could not find;
I set out to find happiness,
Never find it in friendship
It teaches me that each man is for himself;
Then I try relationship
Only to get my heart broken;
Then I found out that love can only,
Be found through the father,
God's only son who died for our sin.
I read The Holy Bible,
And the power of The Holy Spirit guides me.
I found power in the teaching of Christ,
And it empowers me.
Now I see things differently through the word of God.

One fabric

Our religious beliefs, are tearing the fabric
That stitches the human race together,
For the lining of this fabric
Is mended with hate,
That is causing war throughout the world.

We can only have peace
When we can see each other as one family,
The human family;
And find a way to solve our problem
Through, reasoning without prejudice.

That's the only way the fabric,
That holds each thread together permanently
Will stay together,
It's true love that is blinded
To race, religion and the colour of one's skin;

Each nation must find a way to love;
If we continue to let hate surpass love,
Destruction awaits us all,
There is only one true judge He is the Almighty,
Let us put love before all things,
Let us love beyond religion and politics.

Troubled world

A troubled world,
Where hope is built
On uncertainty and speculation,
That has the people in limbo,
Leaders don't have the answers
They are struggling to come up with solutions.

While they fight for power,
Poverty increases,
So the poor rebel,
For their hope are in their leaders hands,
But they don't have the answers, to the problems
That started through greed, Hate and lies.

The truth will never go away
It is like the air we breathe to survive,
It will catch up to you sooner or later,
And it has caught up to the world now,
What will we do?
Turn to the Almighty, or continue to deny
That He is the answer to mankind's problems.

Life's journey

Life is a journey
Enjoy it day by day,
Today you are here
Tomorrow you're gone,
Nothing you will take with you.

Remember Solomon,
The riches king of all,
Remember King David;
All their riches left behind,
But they did find love on their journey,
That love was God.

Everything is just for awhile,
Once a man and twice a child,
The earth was before us
Why take it with you?
It is impossible.

Can you remember?

Can a man count
How many mistakes
He has made in his life?
Can you remember
How many times God has forgiven us?

Each man will make his own mistake,
Some will learn from it,
Some will act foolish and do it again,
But it is God, who judges every man.
He forgives, so who am I
To judge another man.

Before you condemn,
Think how many times,
You have done something wrong.
The man you wanted to kill,
You brag about Him time and time again,
And because he has made a mistake
Death is the answer?

If God should kill
Every time we made a mistake,
How many of us
Would still be walking around?
If we could take the time to see
What we are doing wrong,
This world would be a better place.

Nothing is wrong

Nothing is wrong with having a dream,
Nothing is wrong with having a vision.
Something is wrong,
When you don't try
To put that dream
And that vision into reality.

Don't worry about failure,
Or you will never
Give your dream a chance,
Don't worry about
What people have to say,
Just give your vision a try
You maybe surprised.

If you don't start
You will never finish,
So everything you dream of
Or every vision you have,
Is just an illusion . . . .
So take your step,
Just like a child takes his first step.

We all make mistakes

Mistakes were meant to be,
No one is perfect as you see,
Mistakes were meant to be,
It's a learning tree for you and me.

Sometimes we make mistakes,
Afraid to face tomorrow,
Hoping the world would end,
Or the earth could open up
And take you in,
Feeling so ashamed
That you are no good anymore,
Tear drops rolling down your face.

You say to yourself
How could I do such a thing?
But slowly these feelings start to change
And you just can't believe,
You've been through such a rough time,
What a difference a day can make.

This is the way life is;
Mistakes are for the living
Not for the dead,
As long as there is life,
There will be mistakes
Again and again,
Don't you give up; it's a part of life.

We are one

I see beyond,
The colour of a man's skin;
One blood,
One love,
One God;
You're my brother,
You're my sister.

From Adam comes Eve,
From Eve comes a child (mother of creation)
One man, that is where
We all come from.
One big family,
The human family;

Turn back the clock,
The baby returns,
To the mother,
The mother returns to Adam,
One man stands.
That is where we all come from.

The earth is where Adam comes from,
When we die there we will go also.
If you can see what I see,
Then you will know
God is everything,
The beginning and the end;

REFLECTIONS

GLORY OF THE

Chapter 2

COMING OF

THE LORD

God's wealth

The wealth of this world Comes and goes,
The wealth of God lives forever,
It brings God's wisdom and true love
For all mankind.

What we posses
Goes from hand to hand,
We just have to pass it on
We can't take it with us.

I am thirsty for a taste of God's wealth,
It is not water that I seek,
It is the wealth of everlasting life,
That only comes from God.

This love is above
Human understanding,
It can only be given to you
By God and no other,
It is so pure that man cannot explain it,
Yet it is simple as pure love.

A child

As a child I wanted to be rich,
So my dream was to have it all,
Lots of money, a big house,
Fancy cars and lot of fun,
But life is not like that
It's not an easy road.

They never teach you in school,
About life's ups and downs;
Mathematics and English Just to name a few,
Of the things they say you need,
To get through life,
One of the most important things in life,
Has never been told;

We are obligated to love one another,
Seek God's way of life,
That's the direction every man needs.
We were taught that money,
Can solve life's problems,
That's a lie;
All we need is a happy life with God as our guide.

Love binds all things

Love binds all things together
In perfect unity,
So let yourself be filled with compassion,
Kindness, humility, gentleness and patience.

We must forgive one another
Just as the Lord has forgiven us
And most of all give love
For it's the greatest gift of all.

These are the examples,
We must teach our children,
For without love,
There will be no unity for tomorrow's children,
They will be the men and women of the future.

The things of life

I do not boast about
The things of life,
It is like the rain,
That falls from the sky,
It is here today, gone tomorrow.

When you think,
You're on top of the world,
And everything is going your way,
Don't ever get carried away,
There is always a price to pay.

Give a helping hand,
That your blessings from above
May increase,
And never decrease,
Like the rain that absorbs into the earth.

Why worry when god is in control

Death is certain;
Life is uncertain
So live life to the fullest,
Don't be afraid of death;
Fear God, for He controls
Both life and death,
Don't think about death,
Think about God and do His will,
Why worry when God is in control.

Don't be afraid of death . . .
You're already dead,
For God our master is life
And He gave us life,
So why worry about death?
Seek Him who controls death,
And you will live without fear of death,
Why worry when God is in control.

Try your best at all times,
To walk in the light,
Which death fears and God rules . . . .
From everlasting to everlasting,
The only God, Almighty God,
The King of the universe,
Our true King. Death fears Him,
Why worry when God is in control.

Life is like a hill

Life is like a hill,
A very, very steep hill,
Some people give up along the way,
While others try to reach the top.
You can get there, if you try with all your heart;
Don't think about the steep hill,
Just climb on, the victory will be rewarding.

Always remember, when you fall,
You've got to get up and move on,
Sometimes it's hard when you fall,
And there is no one to give a helping hand,
Remember, God is there with you.

You've got to think positive along the way,
Temptation will be there;
Friends will say you won't make it
But follow your heart;
Be true to yourself.

Thank you lord

There is no room for love
When your heart is filled with hate.

There is no room for peace
When, your heart is filled with war.

There is no room for hate
When, your heart is filled with love.

There is no room for war
When, your heart is filled with peace.

Wisdom is better than weapons of war.

Human love

I found no joy in material things
I found joy in human love.
A gentle touch,
The joy in the eyes of a child
That glows with pure love as gold.

I found happiness
In the voice of human love,
That uplifts the spirit of my soul,
With words of encouragement
To do the best that I can

I found true love,
In the word of God,
That's where he manifests himself,
'Love one another as I love you'
'Forgive as I forgive.'

Love must be the truth,
Truth must be love,
For God is love
And God is the truth
Truth + Love + Forgiveness = God.

The power of god

The power of God,
Can be seen through all things,
That we cannot see with our eyes,
We cannot live without them.
Can you see the air?

We see the sun,
But cannot hold the rays of light,
We see the rainbow,
But cannot hold onto its colours,
We see the moon,
But cannot touch the light that shines.

We see the sea and the ocean,
We see the river and the lake,
But cannot hold onto the water
The sea is blue from a distance,
But when you hold the water in your hands,
The water is colorless and pure.

In the darkest night,
You cannot hold onto the darkness,
In the thickest of fog,
You cannot hold onto the fog,
Some things you will never touch,
But still it exists, so does God.

Today is the day

Today is the day
To love and embrace,
Today is the day
To show love and kindness,
Today is the day
To say 'I love you'
Today is the day to forgive,
For there is no tomorrow.

Love should be given freely
As the air we breathe.
We make excuses
For almost everything,
Even when we must give a little love,
We find a way to hold it inside.
Let love be free.

Walk in love;
Let us not love in words alone,
Neither in tongue
But in deeds and truth,
Love is a free gift
From the Almighty one,
Use it everyday
On this journey of life.

God's love is true love,
It cannot be explained in a lifetime,
It rises above all things,
It cannot be measured,
It has no boundaries,
It cannot be bought or sold,
Love is free to give.
His love is true love.

The place

Take me to a place,
Where the birds fly free
And the wind blows
Between the trees,
And the stream runs free.

Take me to a place,
Where the guns fire no more,
Children playing, having fun
And mothers mourn no more.

Take me to a place,
Where the human race
Sees the water and the wind
As they see the colour of one's skin.

Take me to a place,
Where love is the light
And peace is the ray
That's shine from that light.

Believing in love

Believing in love,
That's the only thing
That keeps me going on
Without love there is no future
Tomorrow's love is the answer
To the healing of the world
For, God is love and love is God.

I give a helping hand,
To my brother in need,
I didn't take the time,
To see the colour of his skin,
It was just a brother in need.

When the world see God,
As a God of love of every colour, class or race,
Then I know there is hope
Of acceptance for all his children.
This world will be a better place,
For you and for me.

To be happy

What can I do to be happy?
Make it your duty to know God,
Look at the trees, the sky, the sun,
The moon and the stars,
See how beautiful they are;
The wind and the rain,
The sea and the ocean;

All the animal and creatures,
Great and small
It is God, who made them all,
That we can enjoy all things on earth
Through His love,
A love that you can see, it's universal.

When you start to know God,
All things before us are meaningless,
Only your brothers and sisters matter;
We are here to love each other,
Just as the Lord loves us,
When you know God,
All things are complete, that is true love.

Spreading god's love

This world we are living in
Is a beautiful world
There is so much to see,
But we are too busy,
Fighting, each other over material things.

God gives me hope,
God gives me strength,
Keeps my dreams alive,
So that I can spread love,
All over the world.

We take no time to watch the sun set,
To see the flowers that bloom,
To walk along a nature trail,
To watch the animals run free
From place to place.

We have no time
To say hello to a friend
To give a child a hug
To smile and say, 'how are you today?'
We have lost it all,
Chasing the rainbow looking for gold.

Little children

Let us love like little children do
Innocent, pure and true.
That is what we should do;
Let us love like little children do,
Unconditionally, pure and true
That is what we have to do.

There is no room for jealousy
In the house of the Lord,
I'm doing the work of my Savior,
Loving and caring for one another,
It's my duty, my only duty.

I have no time to waste
By glorifying myself,
I'm just a humble servant
Doing the Lord's will,
By spreading love to each and everyone,
Regardless of religion, colour or creed.

Love has no colour,
It is pure and true;
We must see beyond religion,
We are the children of God,
We are the human race; religion is tearing us apart,
Let us mend it with love; it is the only true religion.

Be firm

To walk in love, is it difficult?
For whatever you do,
Someone is watching
The things that you do or say
And what you stand for
If you do good or bad,
There is someone to oppose you.

You have to take a stand
And believe in what you do,
For in everything
There are obstacles;
One must be strong in faith
And trust in the Lord.

Be firm in the teaching of Jesus,
Look to him for strength,
He will carry you through this difficult path,
For He is LOVE
So by walking with Him
The walk will be love,
The talk will be love.

Fear the lord

Why is life given to a man
Whose ways are hidden?
What I fear has come upon me,
I have wealth but no health,
It has meant nothing to me.

I'll fear the Lord,
He knows the length of my time
He can extend it, or shorten it,
All things is set before Him,
He is in control.

I know that the Lord is good and great,
So I fear Him;
Try my best to do what is right
That my blessing will be abundant.

Don't you worry

Don't you worry too much about the paper
That wraps the package;
Gently open and see what's inside.
Don't judge from a distance
Try and get close;
You may find, just what you're looking for.
Take it easy, a little patience may pay off,
It is good, to know someone from the inside,
Than judge them from the outside;
You may have just given away gold or silver.

God created man

God created man,
In His own image and likeness,
So what more, do you want to know?
Whenever you see another man,
Show him love.

When you see,
God's own image before you,
Don't be unkind,
He represents God, so love him
The way you would love God,
You've never see God, yet you say you love him.

Love your brother,
Love your sister and you love God,
How blind can you be?
God lives within you and me,
Look and you will see,
Look at the simple things.

True love

True love makes me believe in God.
True love makes me smile each day.
True love carries me through each day.
True love makes me a happy man.
True love makes me who I am.
True love makes me a better person.
True love lets me know am not better than anyone.
True love lets me know that God is real.
True love can change your life around.
True love can make you cry tears of joy.
True love lets me embrace my enemy.
True love protects me, for true love, is God.
True love lets me forgive and forget.
True love takes away all sorrows and brings joy.
True love takes away my pain.
True love makes me give respect.
True love makes me nice to others.
True love conquers all my fears.
True love makes me a child of God.

Be Positive

When the road come to an end,
Turn around and hold
Your head up high,
Don't cry for pity;
Pointing finger blaming someone,
You've got to be strong.

Think positively,
Believe in yourself,
Keep the faith.
Try to see your goals before you,
And you will gain strength,
To move on to better things.

Make that change,
Try something new,
Challenge yourself.
Ask God to give you courage to move on,
Love to give, while
You are going through this change.

Try your best

Troubled times
Will bring the best out of you,
It will bring also the worst out of you,
So in time of trouble you must be patient.

Try your best to listen carefully
And keep faith, it is hard to do,
For all you can think about is your problem,
Nothing else seems to matter.

Problems aren't solved, when you believe
The whole world is against you
And no one cares,
It starts to solve from within you,
That inner peace.

Then you start to see
Things change day by day,
Wonderful thoughts,
A smile on your face, a mind that is clear,
It's only God.

Free spirit

When I feel love flowing through my veins,
And there is no hate in my mind and my heart;
My spirit is free.
My heart doesn't race when I see my brother
From a different nation pass me by,
Then I know; I am free from the heart
Of hate, that tears the soul.

When love flows through me;
Free as the air I breathe,
I let it flow without question,
Then I know, I'm on my way
To the God of love,
That embraces all mankind,
I am free of hate.

When laughter is my weapon and love is my life,
Then I know I am free.
Give me, O Lord, this love,
Then all my troubles will be over,
For love takes it away.
The God of love is my banner.

Forgiveness is love

Some people say what we need is love;
What is love?
When we cannot forgive one another,
It is just a speech
That used to hide the hate from within.

Love starts when you can forgive,
It frees up your heart and soul
And gives you an inner peace;
That releases hate,
And bring God's love within.

I've seen the darkness in me;
It takes God's love to remove it
From the depth of my heart,
And fills it with the light of His love,
That makes me feel free.

Small spaces

I take a ride in an aeroplane,
Looking down from above,
All I see is the beauty
Of God's creation.
Why do we have to fuss and fight?

There is no love,
In those small spaces,
Which men claim to be their homes,
They would die for those spaces;
We are just passing through.

That moment in time,
I spent looking down,
It seemed so calm, in all those spaces.
I hope when this aeroplane lands,
Man would find love and peace, in those spaces.

I see peace,
From above the earth,
But when I come back to earth, to reality,
All I see is hate over love,
War over peace.

The air

There is something that is more precious,
Than silver and gold;
It has never been told.
There is something that is more precious,
Than diamond and pearl;
It has never been told.

The air that we breathe,
Is more precious than anything
Your heart desire,
But you've never been told,
So you pollute and poison the atmosphere.

It is only The Almighty,
That is more precious,
Than the air we breathe;
Seek the way of righteousness
And you will know that the simple things,
In life, mean the most to all.

You can live without,
All these precious stone and jewellery,
But you can't live without the air.
So clean it before it's too late,
Or pay the consequences.

True friend

When the people that you help
Turn their backs on you,
And you feel betrayed,
Don't wish them bad,
Say a prayer instead,
For God knows all things.

Sometimes you go
Out of your way,
To help a friend;
Then find yourself in a jam,
Hoping that you can,
Call on that friend.

Yet the answer is no,
It makes you feel sad,
Even angry inside,
Then you said, 'Time out!
I have to call a true friend."

I bend on my 2 knees,
Close my 2 eyes,
Clasp my 2 hands,
Open my mouth,
And call on my Jesus.
This is my telephone number 2 2 2 1.

This life

I know this life will be over soon,
Should I be sad?
Should I be mad?
What will I gain?
So I give thanks to God instead.

It is reality,
So I've got to do
What I have to do,
Just give love along the way,
Make the best of each day,

Life is nothing but an illusion;
Here today gone tomorrow,
A love that I've lost,
I never will regain,
So love God every day.

To be free

They promise freedom,
While they are slaves
Of destructive habits.
Greed and selfishness
Are on their minds,
For a man is a slave of anything,
That conquers him.

To be free,
You must show love;
To be free,
You must show kindness;
To be free,
You must be truthful.

What is the price for freedom?
Is it silver or gold?
Diamond or pearl?
Or taking another man's life?
What is the price for freedom?
Only God can set you free.

True freedom is Christ.
He died to set us free,
He paid the price,
For you and me,
He shed His blood,
That we may live a life of freedom.

God will provide

With no roof over my head,
I still look to god for shelter;
With no clothes on my back,
I still look to God for comfort;
With no food on my table,
I know God is able to provide for me
As my struggle continue day by day.

O Lord, I ask thee for faith,
For you know all things.
With no one to support me
I look to God instead,
I put my trust in you O Lord,
I know you will provide for me,
You are the source of my life.

GOD IS GOOD ALL THE TIME

Chapter 3

One world

One God,
One World,
One human race.
But like the sun
And the moon
And the star;
To each one
They have their own beauty,
And even among the stars
There are different kinds of beauties.

Black and white,
The only obligation you have
Is to love one another.
Every man, every woman on this earth
Is beautiful in their own way,
And even among mankind
There are different kinds of beauties;
The colour of another man's skin
Is only another beauty
For each and everyone is equal in God's sight.

Love is beautiful,
Love is wonderful,
For love hates no one
Love accepts all colours
Class and race,
Love has no rejection,
It is pure.
Love is eternal;
So without love
We are nothing.

Don't give up the fight

When things go wrong,
As they sometimes will
You have to stay strong.
When the road is rough
And the journey seem so long, take a rest;
Don't give up the fight
Fight on, fight on,
Everything will be alright.

When the funds are low
And the debts are high
Don't you cry;
God is standing by.
Just give him a try,
He is never too busy
To listen to your cry.

When trouble surrounds you
And friends are nowhere to be found;
When you are alone and all you can see
Are the walls tumbling down,
God will pick you up.
He will wipe away your tears
He will give you the strength to carry on.

The meaning of forgiveness

Stop forgiving
From the surface of your heart,
Do it from the depths of your heart,
So this world can be a better place.

There will be no peace in the world,
Until we know,
The meaning of forgiveness;

Remember, when you forgive,
Do it from the bottom of your heart,
God will forgive you too,
For we all make mistakes.

When you make this change
Then the world will heal
If you don't, my children and your children,
Will never, have a world of peace and love.

One family

As the waters are connected,
Springs, rivers, lakes, seas and oceans,
So are the bloodlines
Of the human race.

They are all connected;
We are one big family
No matter where you're from,
We are the earths' greatest gift.

Mankind, the earth is our home
We must look into ourselves
And we will see
That we are connected.

Bread is made for man to eat,
But remember the one that
Put the bread on your table,
He connected us all, He's GOD.

Be humble

When the goodness of life picks you up.
Be humble;
For life has a way of putting us down.
When the blessing of God is upon you,
Be thankful;
For life has a way of putting us down.

When you are riding high,
And the road ahead looks so smooth,
Be nice to the people that you meet along the way;
You may need them.

Don't let success get to your head,
Treat your fellow men with respect;
If you should fall, they would pick you up,
Because of the goodness that you do.

Surprise maybe around the corner;
The road may get bumpy,
The road may get rough,
And you need someone
To give a helping hand,
So be kind and gentle on your journey.

Remember where
You're coming from.
The Lord gives, and
The Lord takes,
He loves the humble, and
Hates the ways of the proud.

Children seek the light

From my balcony,
I watch the children play.
So innocent,
Facing a future that is so bleak,
It makes me weak all over.

Prophecy is fulfilled before my eyes,
Children having children,
Government making promises
Just to control their minds,
Saying that there is a better tomorrow.

Leaders! look to the Almighty,
For wisdom, knowledge and understanding.
God is merciful,
Go down on your knees,
And ask for a solution.

Who is in control

They say the rich control the world.
If you know your Father,
You know it is not so,
This world is God's world,
Which he gave to us all.

Who controls the air we breathe?
The source of life?
Who controls the source of life,
Which is the air we breathe? only God.

I've seen the rich man suffer.
Money could not buy him health,
His riches could never restore his life,
Neither could he take away the poor man's health.

If you open your heart,
And let your heavenly Father's love
Flow through your soul.
You will know that you're wealthy,
From the day you were born.

Hope

The Devil is full of dope,
He takes away our hope;
Makes us unable to cope,
I will cut his rope.
Give my people hope,
Throw away his dope;
No more will I mope,
Jesus brings me hope.

The Devil is full of tricks,
I will not be on the list
In his bag of tricks,
I will have him clipped;
Throw away his tricks,
Then I know that list
Will never exist;

The Devil is full of hate,
I will not hesitate
To close the gate,
That separates hate from love
And war from peace.
Jesus brings me love for my soul,
Jesus brings me hope for a better day.

God is the way

The devil is on a roll,
Man is out of control.
Hate is on the rise,
Love on the low;
Killing on the go,
That's not the way to go.

Teach them to pray,
God is the way;
Listen to what I say,
Don't be a victim,
Stay above the system.

You can live and love,
Or hate and die,
It's up to you.
Tough love, tough love,
It's the way to go.

Tell them the truth,
From they are youths,
Can't spare the rod and spoil the child,
Scold them, scold them.

Word is power

Words are power,
Let us use them positively.
Words are power,
Let us use them wisely.

Word is the force of life,
It is the beginning of the world,
God's spoken words made all things,
Blessed are we, to use his word.

What a privilege
God has given to man
That we could use words and get things done
Oh great is He, so let us give thanks,
Knowing that the word is God,
And God is the word.

Many are too blind,
To see the greatness of God.
We use this power unwisely
To promote hate and not love,
War and not peace.
INSTEAD, we should only promote love.

Equal love

Teachers and leaders,
Remember you are parents too.
Don't you measure love by success
It is wrong.

Elders and Pastors
Remember God choose you to do His work,
Love must be sincere,
Hate what is evil,
Love what is right.

God is just, and will judge
Every man according to His work;
He will never judge
A man by his success;

Equal love for everyone:
Love the shoemaker the same way
As you love the carpenter,
Love the garbage man the same way
As you love the doctor.
LOVE IS MUTUAL!

Darkness overcomes

Darkness overcomes
The children of this world,
For they are living
In the house of hate.
Built on the foundation of wickedness,
Controlled by the master of darkness.

The Devil makes them
Lovers of material things.
They are hunters of vanity,
On a patrol to execute,
Having no mercy for humanity,
They are the generation of vipers.
No love in their hearts,
They are filled with envy.

I'll call on Jesus,
To show them the way to the light,
For there is no other, who exist,
That can change their route
From the road of destruction,
To a life of righteousness.

Prophecy

Some of us
Will have to fulfil prophecy,
Pray not to be like Judas.
If you're stubborn like Jonah,
It doesn't matter,
You still have to fulfil prophecy.

Who will stop the killing?
Nation against nation,
Mother against daughter,
Father against son,
Some of us will have to fulfil prophecy,
Pray not to be like Cain.

Ending of time and they're still out of line,
It's like killing is not a crime.
In this time,
They kill without remorse.
Justice is a thing of the past,
God help us all.

Human love

Try to do good at all times,
It will keep you in the light of God.
Human love,
Is the greatest love in God's sight.

If you put human love
Before all things,
You put God before all things,
Love your neighbour as yourself.

The truth must be above all things,
So is the love of God;
It should be above all things,
Then religion would not blind us.

A little encouragement

All that I ever wanted,
All that I ever dream of;
I owed it all unto you.
You have made sacrifices,
That no one has ever done for me.
You give me hope,
You give me strength
That I can believe in myself.

You've taught me that,
Where there is a will
There is a way.
With faith, nothing is impossible
When you believe in the Lord.
Thank you for sharing your love with me;
Without your love,
I could never go on.

I know the task that set before me,
Is not easy but I'll see it through to the end,
Only because of your love
Why I keep going on,
Your love is a blessing to my life,
What a friend you are to me
Just a little encouragement and love,
Can change anyone life.

A man is a man

What is done, is done,
We can never change the past.
The passed is the past;
But I know for sure
We can make this world a better place,
If we can work together, in love and unity,
Instead of hate and jealousy,
A colour that we must learn to accept;

Every man is the same,
We share the same pain,
And eyes that run tears.
Only God can explain,
Why teardrops roll down our face.
If we take the time to think about each other,
We will know that we are the same.

Ignorance causes us to lose sight of reality,
Fills our eyes with hate and envy,
We will have to accept it, the way it is,
For no man can,
Change the hands of time.

Love in your heart

If you go to bed
With love in your heart,
You will wake up
With love in your thoughts.

Don't go to bed
With hate in your heart,
It will tear you apart.
Try your best to make peace with yourself,
Before you lay your head down
To rest each night;

Tomorrow is another day,
Face it in a positive way.
Ask the Lord to be your guide
In everything that you do.
He will show you the way,
If you trust and believe in Him.

Wait on the Lord for his answer,
Keep the faith;
Always make time to give Him thanks
For He is the one,
That can give you peace and love in your life.

Love overcome

Religion is failing,
Politics is failing;
The hope of the people is dying.
The gospel is the truth
And should be above all things,
Love one another.

Don't kill because of religion,
Don't kill because of politics,
Remember the Ten Commandments.
It was given to us,
That we could live in unity,
It's the truth not religion.

If you love the Almighty God,
You do not love religion,
If you love the Almighty God,
You do not love politics,
All you need to know,
Is that the truth, is God's love.

Who will speak

Tell me who will speak for the children,
I hear them cry,
I watch them die.
The blood of the innocent
Could never be wiped away so easily;
Someone will have to pay one of these days.

God is watching you
Mistreating the children,
A voice that is never heard
In time of war.
They pay the price for things they didn't do,
Good Lord be merciful unto the children.

Mankind is out of control,
It seems as if they've lost their souls,
They use war to solve their problems,
While the children suffer
At their hands.

A good leader

Leaders, do what is right,
Practice what you preach,
For what you sow you will surely reap.
Don't lead my father's sheep astray,
For there is a price, you will have to pay.

Be a good shepherd to His flock,
And your reward will be bountiful,
Take good care and you
Will have no one to fear,
For He will protect you;

Don't let the devil,
Stand in your way, be strong;
God chose you to be His shepherd,
To lead His sheep,
To the promise land;

Teach the children,
About His wonderful work,
Practice what you preach,
For God is watching over you,
So be careful what you do or say.

Keep the faith

When they boast around you,
And say insulting words;
Keep the faith.
Don't lose your cool,
For God loves the humble
And hates the ways of the proud.

God will never bring you down,
But He will bring the proud down,
Don't let hate get the better of you,
Let the love that you have take over.

Show humility,
In everything that you do,
For the one that watches over you
He is humble,
Follow in His work and ways,
And everything will be alright.

Passing through

Man is failing the test of time,
Ignoring the signs of time;
Still committing wars and crimes,
So has it been in the beginning,
So shall it be in the end.

Their hearts are set on material things,
Glorifying the creation and not the creator,
The destruction of man
Is caused through greed and selfishness,
All they do is fuss and fight, pleasing the enemy.

These are the times of tribulation,
You have to put God first,
You can't be blind to hate.
Open your eyes to love, righteousness and peace;
Glorify the Lord in everything that you do.

Don't live to hold on to material things,
We're just passing through;
Just share and care, all that you have,
We're just passing through.

Drugs

What is wrong with you?
You are not the woman
I use to know.
Look what drugs have done to you,
My hope is to hold on to you,
My faith is to wait on you,
My desire is to see you through;
For with God all things are possible.
He will see us through.

I'm losing you to coke,
I'm losing you to crack,
But I'm holding on to you.
People say I'm foolish,
Some say I'm losing my mind,
I should let you go;
But I love you too much
To let you go.

This love is not my love,
It's God's love that keeps me strong.
I'll pay the price
Just to see you right again,
I'll give you all the help I can,
I'll give you all the love that I have.
You were a good woman to me,
Before drugs came into our life,
I'm not giving up on you now.

The finish line

Giving up is a challenge,
That's what keeps me going on each day,
I will never quit.
I'm looking straight ahead,
The winning post is in my mind,
I can see victory at the end.

No time to look back
My mind is made up,
I'm on my way to the finish line.
The odds may be against me
But, there is no room for me,
To stop or think.

I set dead on to this course,
And there is no way
I'm turning back,
For the Lord is with me all the way
I am a winner, with him leading the way,
To the finish line.

God restores

Nothing that a man
Has he will take with him,
But all that he has given,
He will take with him,
All the goodness and love you give,
God will restore for you.

We were born into this world
To enjoy life to the fullest,
But greed and envy
Cause us to lose our way;
So the enemy takes control of us
Blinds us with his lies, pollutes our minds.

Remember all things
Belong to the almighty,
And all He wants from us is that we love him,
Giving thanks, is the sacrifice that honours him,
So fear God and keep his commandments,
For this is the whole duty of man.

Time

Time is what I don't have,
Tomorrow is known to God,
Today is all I live for;
The unknown is in God's hands
Wisdom causes us to know that God
Controls every step a man takes.
Time changes through God's love,
Not man's love,
Time is given, and we can lose it anytime,
Let us glorified God,
With the time He has given us each day.

God's love

Only God can fill the emptiness in your life,
Through unconditional love.
Lord, I feel it inside of me,
It gives me confidence?
To stand tall before all men,
For they are my equal.
My mind is filled with your thoughts.

There is no room for fear
When God fills your heart
With his love,
My mind is filled with God's love;
A love that is seen through actions and deeds,
Not only by talking.

Faith with action,
Is faith with love.
God will set you on the path to success,
If you just keep working.
If you do your part He will do His,
You can rest but never give up,
You can be tired but never quit.

Discover yourself

It is not where you were born
That makes you a better man.
It's the choices that you've made,
And whom you chose to be your mentor.
That's what makes you who you are.

Jesus was born in a manager,
He is the King of Kings and the Lord of Lords.
Moses was born in poverty,
Yet he grow up to be a prince,
And led is people out of slavery.

Try and know who you are,
Seek and you will find.
You've got to be educated to survive
On this journey of life;
You've got to spend time with God,
For time spend with God is never wasted.

I'll never boast

I'll never boast about a living man,
I will talk about the good things
That he has done,
If he is dead
I'll take my chance to boast,
About the things that he has done;

No matter how much,
You really care for someone
You must be on your guard,
Trust only in the Lord,
He will never let you down,
Be careful when it come to secret,
Friend will let you down and break your heart.

Don't tell your best friend
Everything that you do;
Tell it to the Lord.
If you have doubt in a friend,
Follow your heart,
Never worry about,
Telling the Lord anything.
Cry to the Lord, He will listen.

Thank you god

Thank you God, for life,
Thank you God, for a sound mind;
Thank you God, for waking me up
This morning.
Thank you God, for another blessing,
Thank you God, for your grace and mercy;
Thank you God, for EVERYTHING!
Amen.

Time for hope

Try to do what is right,
Open your eyes to the light,
Let's not fuss and fight
For that is not right,
In God sight;
We must unite
and everything will be alright.

We need love,
We need hope,
We need peace,
No time for war.
It's time for love,
It's time for hope,
It's time for peace.

Come together children,
For we are one big family,
Let's join together
And sing songs of love
Before the presence of our father.

God can save

Love can make this world a better place
If we believe in God,
From one man He created all races
And made them live
Throughout the earth,
In Him we live and move and exist,
We are His children, big and small.

Let us come together and join hands
And give Him praise,
For His love is eternal
And will endure to the end.
Give love a try.

We are living in the last and trying days,
Everywhere we turn,
There is war and rumours of war,
There is only one way
We can make our life rich and happy
And that is by love, it is the only answer,
Love is the only way, through Jesus Christ.

Touch of heart

Forgiveness is the true heart of love,
Seek a teacher of heart;
God is a God of love,
He forgives anyone who seeks forgiveness.

Truth must be above all things,
For God is above all things,
Love must be above all things,
For, God is love and love is God.

True love starts when you start to forgive,
That love is God's love.
It holds no grudge and it brings peace within,
It carries no darkness only light.

The light

The world didn't know,
What it had until we lost it;
All we can do is hope and pray.
The world didn't know Him,
Until they crucified Him;

There was a light from Nazareth,
Burning for you and me,
To show us the way that man should follow;
The darkness of men tried to put this light out,
The truth, in this light is pure gold.

No wind can put this light out,
No fuse or chip to be burned out,
It is the light that gives man hope,
And causes the blind man to see,
Any man that sees this light,
Will never be the same.

This light wipes away,
The darkness that sets before us,
Only if we seek this light,
All wickedness will erase from our hearts.
And change us forever.

Try to know god's love

If we could love
Genuinely like God loves us,
What a wonderful world it would be.
I believe the hardest
Thing to do is to love;
And if you find true love,
How can you explain it?

Mistakes are to forgiveness,
As forgiveness is to mistakes,
Love is to God,
As God is to love,
We won't stop making mistakes,
So we will have to forgive
When mistakes are made.
Do you see how hard it is to love?

If you have been accuse of a crime
That you didn't do,
You've been spit on,
Whipped and then crucified.
Before you died,
You forgave every one,
That has done you wrong.

How strong are you to forgive?
How strong are you to love
Someone who've done you wrong,
Like killing your mother or your father?
How strong is your love?
Try and know God,
He is the way to true love.

Tomorrow

Try and understand:
All things before you,
Are nothing but toys to play with and put away.
When the day is over and night takes over,
Then the next day you start all over again.

When you can see all material things this way,
You will start to live life to the fullest,
For we're just passing through;
Nothing to carry on our pilgrim's journey.
If you could only understand life as I see it . . .

I am not looking for tomorrow,
I know tomorrow never comes,
I am laughing as I put these thoughts to paper
And I hope when you read these words
You will understand, that knowing God,
You know tomorrow, for He is tomorrow.